THE CLOUD OF
UNKNOWING

Classics for Everyone

Those who turn to spiritual classics for guidance and inspiration often find their style daunting. The original texts still have much to offer but their diction and idiom, chosen for another era and audience, pose an obstacle to many contemporary readers. "Classics for Everyone" aims to make some of the greatest Christian teachers accessible to all.

THE CLOUD OF UNKNOWING

FOR EVERYONE

ELIZABETH RUTH OBBARD

New City Press
Hyde Park, NY

Published in the United States by New City Press
202 Cardinal Rd., Hyde Park, NY 12538
www.newcitypress.com
©2008 Elizabeth Ruth Obbard

First published in 2007 in Great Britain by
New City, London

Cover design by Durva Correia

Library of Congress Cataloging-in-Publication Data:

The cloud of unknowing : for everyone / [edited by] Elizabeth Ruth Obbard.
    p. cm. --   (Classics for everyone)
    ISBN 978-1-56548-280-7 (pbk. : alk. paper)   1. Mysticism--History--
Middle Ages, 600-1500.   I. Obbard, Elizabeth Ruth,
1945-
    BV5080 . C5 2007
    248.2'2--dc22

                                                            2007028883
Printed in the United States of America

Contents

For the Norwich Diploma Group

"God keeps us always secure,
both in weal and in woe."
(Julian of Norwich)

Introduction

England may well have been thought of as an island of saints during the Anglo Saxon period of her history, but the golden age of English spiritual writing was certainly the fourteenth century when the four best known classics of English spirituality were written, *The Fire of Love* by Richard Rolle, *Revelations of Divine Love* by Julian of Norwich, *The Ladder of Perfection* by Walter Hilton, and the *Cloud of Unknowing* by an anonymous author, probably a priest belonging to a religious order. The interesting thing is that all these books were connected with the solitary life, as was that earlier classic the *Ancrene Riwle* (Rule for Anchoresses). The English were proud of their hermits and anchorites. Something in their way of life seemed to appeal to the English temperament; and those who followed this calling were protected by law and considered an indispensable part of the local scene.

Richard Rolle was a wandering hermit and preacher who died of the plague in 1349. He reminds us of Francis of Assisi in his ability to take the unexpected path, to sing, to love the cross, and to stress the joy he found in freedom of spirit. No institutional religious life for him!

Julian of Norwich, perhaps the best known of the group today (although until recently she was the least known) lived from approximately 1343 to 1413. After a series of visions, or "Shewings," when she thought she was dying at the age of thirty, she retired to an anchor hold beside St. Julian's church and there pondered on what she had seen and understood in those few packed hours as death seemed imminent. Hers is a spirituality that examines deep theological truths. Julian examines sympathetically the problem of sin and evil, ponders on the passion of Jesus as a revelation of love, and on God as Trinity — our Maker, Lover and Keeper. For Julian, God is a God of mercy, a mothering, tender God who wants to be loved and chosen by us in return. She writes, not primarily for professional religious (those who belong to an Order or to the ranks of the clergy) but to give comfort and hope to her even-Christians, ordinary lay folk, as she felt herself to be.

The Ladder of Perfection, for long considered the foremost religious book in English to come out of the period under discussion was the work of an Augustinian canon, Walter Hilton, a priest who belonged to a religious community in Thurgarton, Nottinghamshire. Hilton died in 1396, but apart from that we know nothing about him. He strikes us as a gentle, unassuming person of prayer, well-balanced, and experienced in spiritual direction. His book is intended for an anchoress who has embraced the solitary life after some time as a nun in community. But it is clear that Hilton intends his work to be of help to all who want to follow the path of contemplation by scaling the Ladder that reaches, like Jacob's ladder, between earth and heaven. Hilton is systematic in his teaching and follows the usual practice of encouraging a prayer founded on a love for, and gradual imbibing of, Scripture. His writing is Christo-Centric, as with Rolle and Julian. To know and to love Jesus is the apex of holiness. Humility and love are what matter in the end.

Our own book, *The Cloud of Unknowing,* was written by an unknown author of the fourteenth century, and what a tragedy it is that again we know nothing about him personally. Who was this man with such a grasp of spiritual practice, advising a young twenty-four year-old intending hermit on following the path of contemplative prayer? Unlike our other authors he espouses the *via negativa,* the way of darkness rather than light. He points out that all we can know of God is slight, God in Godself is unknowable by our limited intellect and thought, only love can bridge the gap, a love simple, straightforward, direct, likened to an arrow of love and longing that beats upon the cloud that is the unknown and unknowable God, and ultimately finds its goal. The author speaks too of the way being hard, since between the cloud of unknowing and the self, there must also be placed a cloud of forgetting, where the ego is unable to nourish itself on good memories or indeed any other self-complacent attitude. But this does not happen in a vacuum. Like all orthodox spiritual teachers, our author points out that active love must precede and accompany the way of contemplative prayer. There must be meditation on the life of Christ coupled with works of mercy at the foundational stages or we build on illusion. As with all writings of the English mystics the way is balanced and sane, eschewing all eccentricity and display, as well as harsh penance.

So it will be seen that all these early authors, just beginning to write in the English language (rather than Latin or French) are men and women who are close to us, our spiritual ancestors in the faith. And it is noteworthy that in this case all were linked with the eremitical life in some form. Hilton and the author of the *Cloud* both wrote for intending hermits, while Rolle and Julian followed this form of life, each in their own way, one as a wandering preacher, one as a recluse in the middle of a busy city.

And it is here that I think we can discover their appeal for people now. The medieval hermit or anchoress was not someone whose prime focus was professional religious life. Those who followed this calling were identified with ordinary lay people to a much greater degree than we generally imagine. The hermit was outside the hierarchical structures and power struggles of the Church. He or she was a free spirit, a Catholic Christian identified with the locality, and offering a specific service of prayer and presence when people were in need. The hermit might be a repairer of roads or bridges, a lighthouse keeper, a person who welcomed travelers. The anchorite or anchoress was stable in place, but available as a local counselor, an intercessor for those living in the vicinity.

Interestingly the solitary life is experiencing a new popularity in our own day. Not only does the Church recognize the vocation to solitude outside the parameters of the regular Orders, but the new Canon Law of the Catholic Church makes it possible for the modern day hermit to receive an official consecration. However, today's hermits are seldom as visible as their medieval counterparts. They will certainly be persons whose primary focus is prayer and contemplation "Alone with the Alone," but they may well live in a high rise block in the center of the city, earning a living by simple manual work or counseling, yet retiring to solitude whenever possible, being intercessors who hold the whole world and its needs in their hearts before God. Each hermit is different in that each one is called to respond to grace in a unique way.

So maybe today these authors can speak to where we find ourselves as Christians in the contemporary world. Many feel called to lives of prayer and contemplation, not as members of a religious order but as people on the margins who must find and celebrate their own particular calling among their fellow Christians in times as tumultuous as the fourteenth century.

For the fourteenth century was not a time of peace but indeed of tumult. It was the century of the Hundred Years War, recurring plagues, the Peasants' Revolt, and a papacy divided between claimants in Rome and Avignon. And because the Church was riven by scandal and division it was all the more important that Christians should place their primary focus on a relationship with God rather than expecting the institution to answer all their questions. All our fourteenth century mystical writers show a great respect for the Church as primary teacher and conserver of Christian doctrine, but they themselves were more interested in offering others an alternative vision of prayer and personal relationship with God. Our writers were part of the new literate class that was using the vernacular for the first time to describe religious experience. Personal and individual values and problems were being highlighted. There was a more all-embracing pity for those outside the Church, and a desire to combine the lives of Martha and Mary, symbolic of the active and the contemplative. Better a synthesis than a partisan approach to one or the other. It was the fourteenth century that also saw the growth of the Carthusian Order in England. Everywhere there was a desire to return to a life of simplicity, poverty, solitude, prayer, humility and a conscious imitation of the Savior.

The author of the *Cloud* whose text follows has given us a true English classic, balanced, precise, practical. Although he has in mind a certain young man starting out on the hermit's path, what he has to say can apply to all who feel called to a life of prayer. The very simplicity of his approach is attractive. There is very little structure or progression of thought. All is in the intention, the desire to pierce the cloud of unknowing, the "Cloud" that is God, with an arrow of love and longing that has to be continually directed to its goal.

So our hermit of the *Cloud* is also a pilgrim on a journey, a journey leading into God and sustained by faith. This book is an invitation to become a pilgrim hermit too, together with all those who have walked the path before us.

The Cloud of
Unknowing

Four Degrees of Christian Living

· • • • • • ·

From what I have seen there are four degrees of Christian living:

- ఞ Common
- ఞ Special
- ఞ Singular
- ఞ Perfect

The first three belong to this life; the fourth can begin here but it continues in heaven as well. And as God has led you to desire God in your heart, so God is leading you, it seems to me, toward this way of the perfect.

Most people, yourself included, live an ordinary kind of Christian life. But God has lit a fire of longing in you, a desire to belong to God more completely.

The love which God first put into your heart in creating you, has been the means of God drawing you toward the third manner of living which is called Singular. In this form of living you will learn to lift up the foot of your love, stepping forward confidently toward the last and most perfect degree of Christian life. How God must love you! What a grace is being offered to you!

Learn then to live meekly and in humble gratitude, not thinking that you are better than others just because you are called to solitude. Jesus has chosen you to be one of his beloved flock, and wants to lead you into rich pastures, feeding you with his gentle love while you seek the Kingdom that is your heritage.

Go forward then with confidence, looking forward rather than backward. Do not dwell on what you have achieved so far, but on what you still lack. This will keep you rooted in humility. Fix your mind and heart upon the God who calls you. Guard the windows and doors of your solitude and call humbly upon God in prayer. It is in prayer that God waits for you.

Lifting the Heart to God

• • • • • •

How will you go to God? Let me tell you.

Do not get entangled in things that are temporal and created. Let created things be. They exist in themselves without your constant reference to them. Fix your mind and heart upon God instead. This is a work that not only helps you but helps others in hidden and marvelous ways.

Of course, created things are visible while God is invisible, hidden, as it were, behind a dark cloud of unknowing. So what you have to do is remain in this darkness as long as necessary, just crying out to the One you love. For if you are ever to feel or see God it will be within this darkness.

The Work of the Cloud

• • • • • •

The work that I am talking about is not complicated or long drawn out. It is short and simple and small; so small as to be almost invisible, like an atom.

The human soul has two main powers, knowing and loving. As for knowledge, God is unknowable.

As for love, it is through love that God may be known, but by each person in a different way. Love is the great power behind and within all life.

When grace touches us, our will becomes transformed and we can taste a little of the sweetness of God.

It is for this that we were made in the first place, for love makes our wounded nature whole. If we refuse the work of love then sin takes an ever greater hold on us. As we work at loving we rise higher and higher, away from sin and closer to God.

The Preciousness of Time

• • • • • •

Realize then that time is precious. We can win or lose heaven in an instant. That is why God gives the gift of time moment by moment and not in one big lump. So pay attention to time as it unfolds, and consider what you will do with this precious gift from now on rather than regretting past mistakes.

Surrender yourself to Jesus, the Master of time, and learn from him, from his mother Mary and from the saints, how to use time well by improving yourself and thereby contributing to the whole human community. Jesus, the God-man, knows all about time. He has lived in time too and will be your help.

Just because time comes to you at each separate moment, God can stir your heart with the spark of love many times a day. But you need to be attentive to the Divine spark, not with the mind and imagination, for in that is pride and possible illusion, but in your will, that is, your capacity for love. And this often happens, not in feelings of love, but in darkness, a darkness which I call a "cloud of unknowing."

The cloud I am speaking of is not like a cloud that you see in the sky which brings with it a form of darkness that is easily pierced by light when the sun comes out. The kind of cloud I am talking about is a cloud that signifies a lack of knowing. This lack of knowing includes all your past — all that you have forgotten as well as all you remember — and all that is spiritually unclear. This forms a cloud of unknowing between you and God.

Before you, then, is a cloud of unknowing, and to enter it you must put a cloud of forgetting between yourself and everything else.

Look toward God. Live in life's NOW, not the past or the future. Everything else is fostering illusion.

Practical Advice
On the Work at Hand

* * * * * *

You want to ask "How shall I think about God?" and all I can answer is "I do not know."

You see, no one can actually think of God as we think of created things. All God's works are not Godself. You have to leave them aside and move beyond thought.

And why is this so?

God can only be held close by means of love, not thought.

So do not keep trying to think about God, instead go straight toward the Eternal by placing between yourself and creatures a cloud of forgetting, and turning yourself toward that other cloud, the cloud of unknowing.

Keep your focus by staring at this cloud with a sharp arrow of love and longing, and never turn back from this work, no matter what happens.

If some thought should come to mind while you are attempting to pierce the cloud with your arrow of love and longing, you must say to the thought: "Get down again." Even holy thoughts must be put to one side in this way or you will find yourself being scattered and fragmented interiorly. Simplify your mind, your heart, everything about you and about life, as you direct your arrow Godwards.

Of course, at the beginning of the spiritual life meditation is necessary. We need to be aware of our weaknesses, to think about the kindness of God and the pains of the Passion of Christ. But after a while these meditations need to be put to one side and, like everything else, placed in the cloud of forgetting.

So if you feel called to the work of contemplation by God's grace, let that cloud of forgetting cover all extraneous thoughts, even good thoughts, so that you may pierce the cloud of unknowing with the sharp arrow of love and longing.

One way to help you practically is to choose a word, preferably a word of one syllable such as "God" or "Love." Clasp this word to your heart with a tight band. Make it your shield and spear to beat upon the dark cloud and strike down all other thoughts by driving them into the cloud of forgetting.

Hold on to your sacred word and do not let it go.

Two Forms of
Life in the Church

• • • • • •

Thoughts and imaginings, such as those regarding the life and passion of Christ and the wonderful works of God's creation, can do you good or evil according to how you are in yourself. If having a vivid imagination and a strong intellect make you swollen with pride and empty intellectual curiosity, they are bad. If they turn you toward God in all humility then they can be of help in making progress in the early stages of the spiritual life.

So why are you to press down what may be good under a cloud of forgetting?

The reason is that there are two ways of living the Christian life — the active and the contemplative way, and each have two parts, higher and lower.

The active life is lower than the contemplative life, but having said that, these two ways are joined together so that it is impossible to have one alone; each contains some part of the other.

Those who live the active life must be at least partly contemplative, and those who live a mainly contemplative life cannot neglect the active element. Martha and Mary must work together, but

Mary has chosen the better part that shall never be taken away from her. The troubles and worries of the active life pass, but the contemplative person sits in peace with all things.

The lower part of the active life consists in good, honest works of mercy and charity. By them we are drawn outwards toward others.

The higher part of the active life consists in spiritual meditations on the life and passion of Christ, and in praising God's works. Thus we are moved to live within ourselves in a deeper and more interior way.

The lower part of the contemplative life is likewise in spiritual meditations, but the higher part takes place in darkness, with a loving stirring that reaches blindly toward the mystery of God in Godself. It takes us beyond our limited selves and places us more directly under God.

This is because the contemplative life seeks to attain by grace what we cannot attain by nature alone, namely to be knit to God in spirit, in one love and in one will.

So anyone wanting to reach out to the dark mystery of God, must leave behind, at least for a while, the works of the active life, and send the arrow of love and longing Godwards across the great divide, while placing all other thoughts under the cloud of forgetting.

God is mystery. Any thoughts we may have about God cannot touch the reality. Only love, not thought, can be of help to us here.

Pressing On the
Cloud of Unknowing

• • • • • •

When doing this work of focusing yourself on that arrow of love and longing directed to the dark cloud of God, take no notice whatever of any thoughts or images that may surface during that time. Believe me, the work of secret pressing on the cloud of unknowing is more beneficial to yourself and to others you may want to pray for, than any acts of the imagination, however holy.

Lift your love to the cloud.

Place all else behind and beneath you.

Thoughts that come unbidden to your mind are not sinful, but they can hinder you from rooting yourself purely in God, thus destroying your peace.

Learn to discern where your thoughts come from and where they may lead you. A lot of things are a waste of time and energy. Be aware of what passes in your heart but don't follow it up. Leave thoughts alone.

Another illusion is to think that a lot of hard penance will purify you and bring you close to God. A hard bed, coarse clothes, early rising, even bodily mutilation are of no help whatsoever. These things in themselves do not get rid of sin. Neither do holy meditations, on their own, take you far along the path you want to travel.

The better part, that of Mary, is what matters in the end. Only God can destroy the roots of sin and make us holy. It is not something you can achieve by yourself, however hard you try. So relax! Don't get all uptight about making progress.

Humility and love are the basis of everything. If you have these you have all that is necessary, and these are gifts from God. They come as a grace, not as a reward for effort.

The Gift of Humility
or Meekness

• • • • • •

Humility is knowing ourselves as we really are, and knowing God as the One who is All.

Imperfect humility, the first step toward true humility, is to have a proper knowledge of ourselves. This is worth laboring for, as it brings along with it a knowledge of God such as can be felt in our mortal body.

Perfect humility, however, is not about an awareness of our own wretchedness. If that were so, then Jesus, Mary and the saints could not be termed truly humble.

And if we look at Mary (Magdalen) we know that her sins did not keep her back from God and mired in her own sorrow. Instead she hung up her love and longing in the cloud of unknowing and learned the secret of real love, a love rooted in God moment by moment.

Martha and Mary

· ● ● ● ● ● ·

Luke's Gospel tells us of two sisters, Martha and Mary. Mary sat at the Lord's feet while her sister Martha was busy preparing a meal.

Even though Martha was doing a good and holy work by serving Jesus, Mary was attentive to the essence of Christ her Savior, sitting in absolute stillness, oblivious to all around her, with her secret love pressing upon the high cloud of unknowing between herself and God.

Nobody in this life can be so perfect that there will not be a large cloud of unknowing between themselves and God. This was the cloud occupied by Mary. And even when her sister complained, Mary continued to sit in perfect stillness, paying no attention to Martha's words.

Martha, the symbol of the active life, stands for those active persons who complain about contemplative persons even today. It seems to them that contemplatives are doing nothing and opening themselves to grave faults. In the eyes of modern Martha's, to be busy is to be good!

Of course, nobody is faultless, and contemplatives have failed often in the past, becoming hypocrites or being embroiled in other mischief. However, this is not what I want to speak of here.

Martha is not to be condemned. Her complaint was justified in the circumstances in which she made it. She spoke courteously, but she did not understand the calling of Mary, which was different from her own.

In the same way, people today are prone to complain against those who are pursuing a contemplative way of life, not through malice, but because they do not understand it. It seems a useless waste of precious time.

Mary is our example here. Jesus answered Martha on her behalf, while Mary remained in peace and quiet.

"Martha, Martha," said Jesus, "You are very busy and occupied with many things." Good things, yes, helpful things, yes. But ultimately "Only one thing is necessary."

And that one thing is what Mary has chosen, the stirring of love that shall last in eternal bliss, and "shall not be taken away from her."

Mary Has Chosen
the Better Part

• • • • • •

The active and contemplative life intermingles in various degrees, but the higher part of the contemplative life is the "best part" of Mary. Note that Mary did not choose the best LIFE, because there are only two lives, the active and contemplative, and of these two no one may choose the best by themselves. But of these two lives Mary has chosen the best PART, and this shall not be taken away from her.

The first and second parts of the active life are temporary and concerned with the here and now. We must sorrow over our sins, feed the hungry, clothe the naked, visit the sick and imprisoned, bury the dead. But in the part that is best, none of these things will be necessary.

Those whom God calls by grace to the contemplative life do not follow their own choice but God's choice of them. To this they should respond with all their energy, and others should respect that calling and leave them to follow it in tranquility.

It was to Mary that Jesus appeared after his resurrection. Between them was a deep and overwhelming love that transformed the sinfulness of her past and made of her the one best beloved.

If we make our own love and life conform as far as possible to the love and life of Mary, Jesus will speak on our behalf, and having him, we will need nothing else.

The Meaning and
Work of Charity

• • • • • •

As humility is understood and taken for granted as a basic attitude when we beat upon the cloud of unknowing, forgetting all else in the process, the same holds for charity.

Charity signifies nothing else except love of God, love of others, and a true love of self. God must be loved for Godself, and the substance of this work of love is having a naked intent directed toward God alone, that arrow of love and longing I have spoken about.

Love does not seek to be free from pain or to receive greater rewards. Love seeks nothing but God.

As to love of others, in this work of intent longing for God, all are loved and cherished equally. Good is willed indiscriminately to all, even, and especially, to those who hurt us.

Working to have a naked intent upon God means not distinguishing in our love between friend and foe, relative and stranger. That doesn't mean of course that we will not feel a special affection for some people (even Jesus had his special friends on earth). But while at prayer all are to be loved equally, for we are all members of the one Body of Christ, saved and redeemed by his Passion.

The Need for Grace

· • • • • • ·

We need God's grace to persevere in beating upon the cloud of unknowing in prayer. It is a difficult task. Why is that?

Because it demands that we tread down all remembrance of created things, holding them beneath the cloud of forgetting. This is our fundamental struggle. The stirrings of love that may occur are not of our own making but come only from God as and when God wills. If we go on with our work, we can be sure that God will not fail to do the Divine part of it. But we need to know how to wait, and not force progress before the time is right.

So move steadfastly ahead. Labor hard, then the difficulty of this work will ease off with practice. Soon God will begin to take over more and more, sometimes allowing a beam of spiritual light to pierce the cloud of unknowing between you and Godself. At other times God will lead you along secret paths or touch your feelings with the fire of love. What matters is the work that you must do.

Leave the rest to God.

Saints and Sinners

. . . . . .

Those called to the contemplative life are those called to work in this special way. So the first step is to have a clean conscience and a strong desire to resist sin. Even so, it is extremely difficult to remain before the cloud of unknowing because we are taken up with created reality insinuating itself between ourselves and the reality of God.

Patience and meekness are required before we reach the purity of soul that God wants for us. However, sometimes through God's grace, sinners can reach perfection quicker than those who seem to have sinned less. And all this is through the mercy of God who is no respecter of persons. On the Day of Judgment no doubt some whom we considered sinners will sit side by side with the saints, while others, who at present are thought of as holy, will find themselves cast out. You see from this that no one should judge another in this life. Deeds may be good or evil, but the person cannot be judged as being good or evil. Only God is the judge of that.

Only someone truly touched and enlightened by the Holy Spirit is able to form a proper opinion of others. Meanwhile, the safest course is to look to your own behavior and leave others alone! Anything else is very dicey!

Once you have done what you can about purifying your own conscience, take no notice of past sins that come to mind. Place them under the cloud of forgetting; and if that seems difficult, develop some tricks or private techniques to help yourself along. Meanwhile I will share with you what I have found to be one of the greatest helps on this path.

One help is to look past the distracting memories of sins committed as if you were looking over your shoulder at something beyond, that is, to God.

Another way is to stop fighting these thoughts and just let them pass over you while you yourself remain before God in peace.

Realize and accept your weakness and in this way you will overcome it. Continually fighting your weakness is a waste of energy, and a distraction from your real work.

So labor peacefully and steadfastly. Have your testing time now rather than hereafter. Accept your weakness as being part of who you are, one of an imperfect human race. Do not let sin have power over you, either past sins or present ones. Leave all in God's hands.

God Our True Teacher

● ● ● ● ● ●

Alas, I cannot tell you myself how you can come to this work of entering the cloud of unknowing because it is all God's work, and has nothing to do with natural gifts or merits. God is merciful and works how and when and in whatever way God wants.

This grace is not given as a reward for innocence, nor withheld because of past sinfulness. Indeed, I believe that God will often give this grace to those who have sinned much, rather than to those who have been relatively good. No one is debarred, for all are capable of receiving the special grace of God which will enable them to begin the work of contemplation if and when God wishes to grant it.

Be humble and open, not puffed up with pride. Desire with true desire and you will receive. God gives the grace for what we really want. Be docile to God's stirrings within rather than making plans of your own. Passivity rather than activity is required at this stage, enabling you to follow wherever God leads.

You are the tree, God's gift the caretaker.

You are the house, God's gift the dweller within it.

Don't try to think and reason things out at this stage, walk instead with confidence in the darkness where God dwells.

Trust that God is working within you in the stirrings you feel, and try not to analyze these too closely.

Methods of Prayer

Learning to pray has three parts:

- ❧ Reading
- ❧ Thinking
- ❧ Praying

For beginners and those progressing along the way of prayer the stage of thinking can only be reached after reading and hearing the Word of God. Prayer cannot happen without first thinking about God's word, either written or spoken.

God's word is like a mirror. If you have a dirty mark on your face you can only see it if you look into a mirror or someone else tells you about it. In the same way it is by reading and hearing God's word that you become conscious of sin. It is so easy to be blind to a dirty mark, physical or spiritual, but once you are aware of it then you want to wash it off. If the mark is a one-time sin then the well is holy Church and the water is confession. But if the mark is a deep-rooted sin, then the well is the mercy of God and the water is prayer and all that prayer involves. Praying just cannot be attained without going by the path of prior thinking.

However, for those who are on the way to contemplation, thinking and praying have been practiced over a long period and have become a kind of second skin. At this point there is much more spontaneity. For example, just the word SIN is enough to start you off without further analysis. You don't need to go into details, just behold sin in itself as a whole.

Just as those who follow the contemplative path preparing the ground by thinking, so their praying follows a similar path. Yes, they pray the prayers ordained by the Church; but as for other prayers these rise spontaneously to God without having been planned in advance.

Such prayers are usually wordless, or at most a few syllables — the shorter the better. When anyone is in danger of fire, or some other emergency, they just cry out a word like "HELP!" from the depths of their being. Shortness and abruptness sum up the need far more than lengthy explanations.

One word like "FIRE!" or "HELP!" alerts others quickly to what is happening. Just so, one little word like "GOD" or "LOVE" pierces heaven far more swiftly than a whole set of mumbled psalms.

The Value of Short Prayers

· • • • • • ·

Why does short prayer of one syllable have such power?

Surely it is because the one who prays in this way puts into that word the whole of themselves.

If someone you disliked called out "Help!" or "Fire!" pity would be stirred in your heart simply because a fellow human being was in distress. If we are merciful in responding to others, even if they are our enemies, surely God will not be less merciful or less attentive to the cry of the poor.

So the way to pray is that which compresses your whole being in the simplicity of one syllable.

What should that one word be for you? Well, first look at the nature of prayer, which is a devout intention directed toward God. The word "Sin" encompasses the whole gamut of evil when we wish to remove it from our hearts, so the word "God" can encompass all that we mean when we desire the Good.

Feel free to respond to grace in this matter, but keep your words simple and direct, and of one syllable if possible. The prayer may be brief but if it is frequent God will come to your aid. Make that one word a cry of love and longing, going like an arrow straight to the heart of God.

What does it matter what kind or how many sins are on your conscience? All sin is equally vile because it separates you from God. So just feel sin to be one lump and cry out simply "Sin, sin, sin! Out, out, out!" You don't have to consider sin in any detail. God will teach you to cry out simply, and without even pronouncing the word except when it literally bursts out from you in fullness of spirit.

Likewise the word "God." Fill yourself with its spiritual meaning without thinking of God's attributes or works. In having God you have all Good. Just want God, intend God, and leave all else alone.

Alternate the words "God" and "Sin." For sin will always be with you to some extent in this life.

Remember the basics:

- ☙ If you have God, you will have no sin.
- ☙ If you have no sin, you will have God.

Using Discretion

As far as prayer goes, keep my advice strictly without making any exceptions. As for other things, use your common sense in eating, drinking, protecting your body from extremes of heat and cold, relating with others, and so on.

Whatever you are doing, the river of prayer should be flowing either above or underground, peacefully and calmly. So be prudent as regards care of your body; good health is a gift to be preserved. If sickness should come to you, be patient, and wait for God's mercy. Patience in sickness is often more profitable than fulsome devotion practiced in good health.

If you want me to give you rules about your food or sleep, all I can say is "do the best you can." Perseverance in prayer will give you the right guidelines on all outward things. Freedom consists in not being overly concerned about other elements in your life. Too much attention to minutiae takes your mind away from the work at hand, which is continual prayer. So just keep lifting your heart with a blind stirring of love, thinking of sin or of God. Want God. Avoid sin. Everything is summed up in these two words.

The Secret of
Self-Forgetfulness

Apart from God, tread all else down under the cloud of forgetting: yourself, your actions, those of other people, and all useless memories and thoughts. A perfect lover is self-forgetful, thinking only of the beloved.

So set aside all else that is racing around in your mind and heart and concentrate on God. Thinking about self is bound to be depressing because of your sinfulness; and even when sin is behind you there will always remain some feelings which need to be overcome before this work is made steadfast and perfect in you.

Getting beyond yourself and your subjective feelings is a grace springing from a deep spiritual source. Just existing is cause for existential sorrow. Knowing and experiencing God as your only true joy will surmount your deeply felt pain.

This doesn't mean ingratitude for the great gift of life that God has given. In all our sorrows we still want to exist, but we do not want to feel our being intruding in the work of prayer, and getting in the way of God.

Everyone called to contemplation needs to feel sorrow for sin and desire for God. Apart from that, let God teach you according to your abilities and gifts.

Don't try and do it all yourself. Be humble. Seek advice.

Do not strain yourself or you will become exhausted. Attend to the movements of grace rather than trying to force them. If you use force you will only wear yourself out and then have to seek other forms of diversion.

The fire of love and the fire of sensuality are closely related. False feelings, false knowledge, are all too evident in some. The devil too has his contemplatives in thrall! Make sure you are not one of them!

Avoiding Deceptions

· ● ● ● ● ● ·

Never try to achieve anything by brute force. Desire for God involves patience and humility above all. Using brute strength is like wrestling with flying stones. They hurt where they hit. Violence breeds violence. Patience breeds mildness and gentleness both of body and soul, like a child resting peacefully in the arms of its mother. So do not try and force yourself upon God by violent means. Let God discover your longings in God's own good time.

As you know, God is Spirit. Therefore it is by spirit that you will be united to God, not by physical effort. Look deeper into yourself and discover your longings there. Enjoy a little hide-and-seek with God. Don't be continually "up front"; let things move to a more interior level. Heart speaks to heart in silence.

Serving God
in Body and Spirit

‣ ● ● ● ● ● ‣

God wants to be served with both body and spirit. Both are part of your humanity and both will share in your ultimate reward. Do not despise bodily pleasures given by God; you need them to enjoy life's beauty and goodness. Other more directly spiritual pleasures can also touch the senses. Again, receive them with gratitude, not trying to hold on to them if and when they pass.

Beware, however, of other feelings that touch your senses but seem to arise from nowhere in particular. Do not go along with everything you hear and see, and keep yourself interiorly calm. Other pleasures can be good or evil, but I am not going to spend time writing about all that here. Others have done a better job in other books.

Just keep the blind stirring of love going within you, sending your arrows of love and longing Godwards, and leaving all else alone. This stirring of love will be a sure guide for good living.

Do not waste time on passing things, and do not rely on what you feel. Feelings come and go and are not a reliable guide. The weak and the strong need different treatment, which God knows how to give. Some are led by one way, some by another according to their strength and natural dispositions. Just direct your attention and your hope to the blind stirring of love within. Keep going. Keep calm. Keep your heart steadfast in God, and forget the rest.

Watch Out for
Two Little Words

• • • • • •

Now I have to speak about two little words that are easily misunderstood. These words are "in" and "up."

In

It is common knowledge that when young disciples want to give themselves completely to God, they begin with some penance, prayer, reading, and so forth. The next step is that they hear about the inner work I have been speaking of and they are curious to know more.

If those who are directing such persons advise against beginning this work too soon, their disciples are quick to complain. They believe themselves to be further on than they are, and they abandon the practices they should continue to follow as beginners. In this way they work against nature and are in league with the enemy.

They turn inwards in a great hurry to reach perfection before they are ready for this step. They huff and puff and strain themselves in their efforts to see what is IN them. Their brains go round and round, causing them to think they are truly "in" themselves and "in" God. It is all illusion! And the devil lets them carry on in this way.

All sorts of physical eccentricities enter into the bearing of people straining to go "in" before it is time for them to do so. It would make *anyone laugh to see* them all stressed out about this for nothing! Those who really follow God's inner workings are agreeable in bodily bearing, being both relaxed and spiritually attractive. Their words are restrained. They eschew any sham in their actions. They are not interested in seeming holy but in actually being holy. They are who they are in all simplicity, and have nothing to do with the acting out that leads hypocrites astray. Beginners can fail by having too much zeal in correcting the faults of others rather than seeing their own. They think the fire of God's love rules their lives, whereas, if truth be told, it is the fire of hell that motivates them. They are always on the lookout for others going wrong or doing wrong.

Others fail through too much emphasis on the mind. They want to know and understand everything, and are easily led down wrong paths simply because such paths are relatively easy and human nature is naturally lazy.

Look "in" in the right way. Stay at peace, and do not try to rush the process. You may stir up more trouble than you can handle.

Up

Now we shall see how beginners misunderstand the word "up." When they hear such words as "Lift up your hearts to God" they immediately begin to stare at the stars as though they were already hearing the song of the angels in heaven. They fashion a kind of interior telescope to pierce the clouds, in the hope that they will find God sitting on a throne "up there" somewhere.

Their imagination conjures up angels playing musical instruments. They consider a special dew to be manna from heaven, and sit waiting to receive it with open mouths, as if they were catching flies! Yes, Christ Jesus is in heaven. That is all we need to know. Otherwise leave "heaven" alone and attend to your work here below.

Heaven is not about being "up" in a physical way. Jesus ascended into heaven to be sure, but we are not to keep our gaze fixed on the stars, or strain our imagination in order to follow him there. Heaven is not "up" at all in a physical sense. To be spiritually in heaven is not about "up" or "down," one side or another side. It is where our love and desire are. We live where we love in the here and now.

The Powers of the Soul

· ● ● ● ● ● ·

Memory is the main power within us. It encompasses all we do and understand, although it does no work of itself.

Apart from memory we have two principal working powers in our soul and two secondary powers. The two principal powers are understanding and will. The two secondary powers, which are linked to the body, are imagination and our bodily senses.

Understanding shows us good and evil. The *will* enables us to choose the good. *Imagination* brings things to mind while *bodily* senses make us aware of pleasure and pain.

Imagination never stops working away, but if we are to pray well it needs to be restrained or it will run away with us.

Bodily senses need to be governed by the will or they will take on a life of their own. Our bodily senses like and want pleasant things, which are not necessarily good things.

So keep your imagination on a leash and plunge yourself into the pure presence of God.

Do not try and feed your inner life on physical things. Be willing to remain in darkness.

It is hard to continue the work of prayer when there is no felt feedback, so hold on to this truth: there will always be a "cloud of unknowing" between you and the God who is Mystery.

That is why you must keep at your inner work which does not depend on sense or feeling, and for some it will come more easily than for others.

Moses, Aaron and Bezaleel

• • • • • • •

Let us look at Moses the leader of the Hebrew people, his brother Aaron the priest, and Bezaleel the maker of the Ark of the Covenant, to illustrate what I want to say at this point.

The Ark of the Covenant is a symbol of contemplation under the Old Law, and contemplatives are those who look after the Ark. The Ark contained all the treasures of the temple, just as our little love, concentrated on the cloud that is God, holds within it all good things and is God's spiritual temple.

Before Moses could discover how the Ark was to be made he had to climb the mountain with great effort, and remain there working in the cloud of God's silent presence for seven days before God showed him the Ark's pattern. So Moses stands for those who have to make strenuous efforts to complete their spiritual work, and even then their experience of God depends on God's condescension and may well be infrequent. All is grace, not earned reward, despite their efforts.

Aaron, on the other hand, because he was a priest, could enter into the temple whenever he wanted and have access to God as often as he liked. Aaron therefore stands for those who by their spiritual wisdom, aided by God's grace, can achieve perfect contemplation at will.

Each one of us has to follow our own unique path and cannot judge others by our own particular experience, as if it were the one measure for all to be measured against. And of course, as God is sovereignly free in giving gifts, it may be that those who begin with great effort, like Moses, may in time attain to perfect contemplation whenever they will.

The third person in the story of the Ark is Bezaleel who made it according to the pattern shown to Moses by God. He made the Ark by his own skill but was assisted by the instructions given to Moses on the mountain.

I am like Bezaleel in you, my dear friend, in a sense directing your hands in the building of this Ark. But if you want to be an Aaron with unimpeded access to the Ark, then work hard and do what God wants you to do in your own call to the contemplative life.

If the way I have been describing does not fit your particular temperament you may take some other way to God without any blame.

But I think that the more you read what I have written the more you will feel that this way is for you, because I discern that it is in close harmony with who you are and who you want to be.

Final Words

• • • • • •

Do you want to discover whether God has really called you to this work of contemplation? Then ask yourself whether you feel attracted by what I have written and are willing and ready to practice sending Godwards this little arrow of love and longing that presses on the cloud of unknowing.

With merciful eyes God looks not upon what you are or what you have been, but on what you want to be. God looks at your desires. Those who want God will have God.

Desires are what count. What do you want now? Not what have you done in the past?

If you desire God then go forward with confidence. Farewell my dear friend for whom I have written this book. Peace, wisdom and spiritual comfort be yours, with all the grace that belongs to those who love God.

For Further Reading

Texts

The Cloud of Unknowing, Edited with an Introduction by James Walsh S.J., Classics of Western Spirituality Series, SPCK 1981.

The Cloud of Unknowing, Translated and introduced by Clifton Wolters. Penguin Classics 1961.

The Cloud of Unknowing, Introductory commentary and translation by Ira Progoff, Rider & Company 1959.

General Works

Belisle, P.D., *The Language of Silence — The Changing Face of Monastic Solitude*, Darton Longman & Todd 2003.

Coleman, T.W., *English Mystics of the Fourteenth Century*, Epworth Press 1938.

Cox, M., A *Handbook of Christian Mysticism*, Crucible 1983.

Glasscoe, M. (ed.), *The Medieval Mystical Tradition in England*, D.S. Brewer 1987.

Knowles, D., *The English Mystical Tradition,* Burns & Oates 1961.

Nuth, J.M., *God's Lovers in an Age of Anxiety*, Darton Longman & Todd 2001.

Thornton, M., *English Spirituality*, SPCK 1963.

Also available in the same series:

**Teresa of Avila's *The Way of Perfection*
*... for Everyone***

Elizabeth Ruth Obbard

64 pages, paperback
ISBN: 978-1-56548-262-3

**Thérèse of Lisieux's "Little Way"
*... for Everyone***

Elizabeth Ruth Obbard

72 pages, paperback
ISBN: 978-1-56548-272-2

**John of the Cross' *Living Flame of Love*
*... for Everyone***

Elizabeth Ruth Obbard

72 pages, paperback
ISBN 978-1-56548-267-8

To order call 1-800-462-5980
or e-mail orders@newcitypress.com